THE VICTORIAN COUNTRY HOUSE

In the late nineteenth century, during Queen Victoria's reign, many rich people spent a large part of every year living in big houses in the countryside. As well as being a family home, the country house was a place to entertain guests who lived in London and other large towns.

There were no vacuum cleaners, washing machines or other labour-saving devices, so most household tasks had to be done by hand. Rich Victorians expected almost everything to be done for them, and a big house needed lots of servants. Housemaids cleaned the rooms and lit the coal fires. Footmen answered the front door and served the meals. Ladies' maids and valets helped their employers dress in the mornings and undress at night. In this book, we look at a day in just one part of the country house – the kitchen.

▲ A typical Victorian town house, owned by a lower middle-class family. Even houses like this had servants to do much of the work.

▼ Think of all the work needed to run a big country house like this one. Every room used by the family had a coal fire, made every day by a housemaid.

WHO WORKED IN THE KITCHEN?

Some servants in the house were more important than others. At the bottom, there were children, such as the odd-job boy who cleaned the boots and polished the knives. Above them there were the housemaids and footmen. Two servants were at the very top: the butler, who was in charge of all the male servants, and the housekeeper, who was in charge of the female staff.

The housekeeper gave orders to the cook, who was usually in her thirties or forties. She ran the kitchen and did the complicated cooking jobs. Victorian newspaper cartoons often made fun of cooks, showing them as fat, bad-tempered women who drank too much.

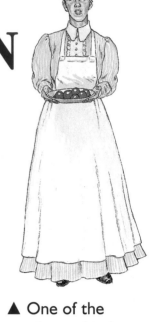

▲ One of the two lower kitchen maids. She is 17.

▶ This is the odd-job boy. He is 10 years old and has just left school and started working full-time at the house. He began working when he was 8, helping his father who looks after the stables.

◀ The scullery maid, aged 10, peels potatoes.

◀ The second lower kitchen maid, who is 16, guts and cleans fish, ready for cooking.

The cook had three assistants. There was the upper kitchen maid, normally in her twenties, who was learning to be a cook. She was helped by two lower kitchen maids, who were in their teens. One kitchen maid described her work: *'My job other than cleaning was to prepare and cook the vegetables and learn to make sauces, sometimes three or four different ones with a seven-course dinner, but as cook was so often drunk, I had to do a lot more.'*

▲ This early Victorian housekeeper was called Mrs Garnett. The fact that her employers wanted a portrait of her shows how much rich people valued their housekeepers.

The youngest servant of all was the scullery maid, aged between eight and 12. She did all the washing-up, in the room called the scullery. She also washed and peeled vegetables and plucked birds. If she worked hard, she might become a kitchen maid in a year or two.

The housekeeper was usually a woman in her forties or fifties. She kept the accounts, hired and fired the maids and organized the shopping. She had to make sure there was no waste or theft, and she was very strict.

▶ The cook is 48. She has worked in kitchens all her life, starting as a scullery maid when she was eight.

▶ The upper kitchen maid is 22. She is helping the cook to make a pie.

THE VICTORIAN KITCHEN

Servants and their rich employers lived very different lives, in different parts of the house. The servants' rooms, such as the kitchen and the hall where they ate, were mostly on the ground floor or in the basement. For this reason, their part of the house was called 'below stairs.'

The family ate upstairs, in the grand dining room. There were even special servants' staircases at the back of the house, to prevent the family and their staff from meeting unexpectedly.

Because the kitchen was often hot, it had to be in the coolest part of the house. In a country house, this was the north-east corner, away from the afternoon sun. The room had a high ceiling which helped to stop it getting too hot and stuffy, and there were big windows to let in plenty of light.

The kitchen was used only for cooking meals. There were other rooms for storing food. Foods that went off, such as fish and meat, were stored in cool rooms called larders.

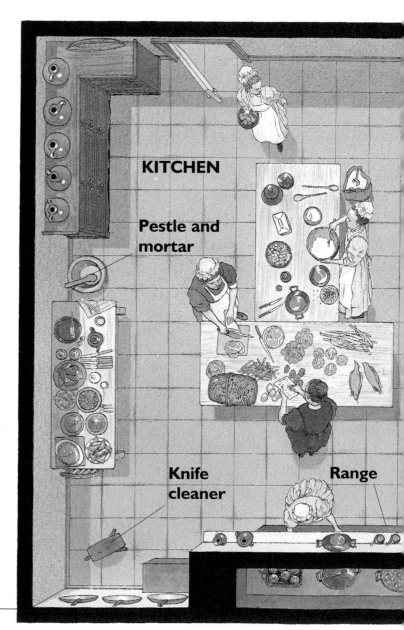

▼ The housekeeper (in the red dress), making her daily visit to the kitchen, gives the day's orders to the cook.

KITCHEN

Pestle and mortar

Knife cleaner

Range

▶ This plan shows the layout of the service wing, and where it is in relation to the rest of the house.

The housekeeper's storeroom, which was a little warmer, contained all the things that had to be kept dry, such as tea, sugar and spices.

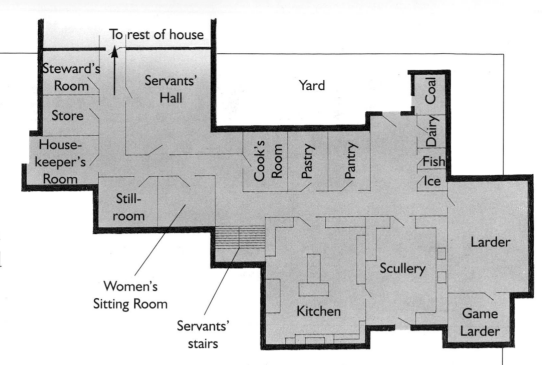

There was also a still-room, for making jam, and a dairy, for making and storing butter and cheese.

Next to the kitchen was the scullery, where the scullery maid did the washing-up and peeled the vegetables. Having a separate scullery stopped the kitchen floor becoming wet and slippery, and kept the dirt away from the food.

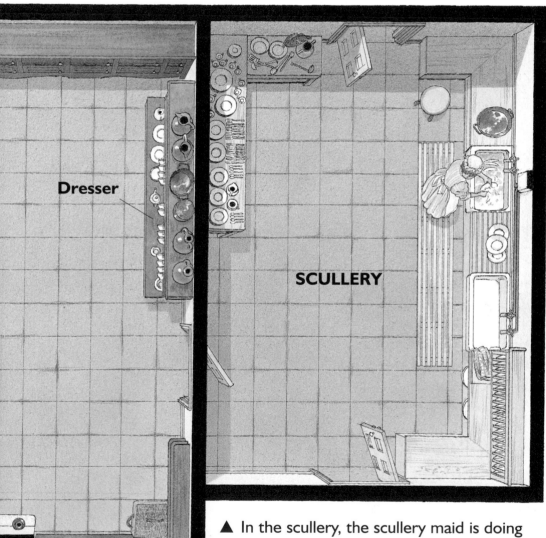

▲ In the scullery, the scullery maid is doing the washing up. She stands on raised wooden slats, which stop her slipping on the wet floor.

KITCHEN EQUIPMENT

The most important piece of kitchen equipment was the big iron range, where all the cooking was done. A range was like a modern cooker, except that it burned coal in a central fire. On either side of the fire, there were ovens, for roasting and baking. The top was used for boiling, frying and broiling (grilling over the flames). The range was also used to heat water in a boiler.

▲ A collection of Victorian kitchen equipment. How many of these can you identify?

The coal fire made a lot of work for the kitchen maids. Every morning, before a new fire could be lit, they had to sweep out the ash and scrub the range clean. Then they dried it and rubbed it with black polish until it gleamed.

▼ Before stainless steel was invented, knives needed polishing once a week. This was done in a machine with a revolving drum. The odd-job boy turned a handle which rubbed the knives with rough bristles and soft cloths.

There were dozens of different shaped pots and pans, made of gleaming copper or black cast iron. Each pan had its own special use. For example, there were two types of pan just for poaching fish: a long, narrow fish kettle for long, narrow fish and a low, wide turbot kettle, for cooking flat fish. The bain-marie sat on top of the range. It was big enough to hold several pots and pans, which stood in hot water to keep cooked food hot until it was time to serve it. There were also many small kitchen tools – knives, whisks, measuring jugs, rolling pins and mixing bowls.

Finally, there were three other things that every kitchen needed: a clock on the wall, to time the cooking of the dishes; a set of scales, to weigh the ingredients; and at least one book of recipes. Cooks bought printed cookery books and they also copied recipes from newspapers.

▲ A Victorian kitchen range. An enclosed coal fire in the centre heated the ovens on either side and the hot plates on the top.

▲ There were kitchen machines for grinding and mincing, and cleaning knives, but they all had to be worked by hand.

▼ Here you can see just some of the equipment used every day in the kitchen. The upper kitchen maid has been making sausages. She has flavoured the sausage mixture with spices, kept in the box. Meanwhile, one of the lower kitchen maids is making jelly using copper moulds.

SUPPLIES

Much of the food prepared in the kitchen came from the land belonging to the house. There was an an orchard, a garden and a greenhouse, where the gardener grew fruit, vegetables and herbs. The surrounding countryside was a good source of game – wild animals that were hunted for sport.

Autumn and winter was the shooting season, when rich Victorians hunted deer and game birds such as pheasants and woodcocks. These were stored in the game larder, where they were left hanging for several days before cooking. This helped to make the meat more tender and gave it a stronger flavour.

▶ Here are just some of the supplies brought to the kitchen. The object at the bottom is white sugar, which was sold as a hard cone.

Other supplies were ordered from tradesmen in the nearest town, and delivered to the kitchen by horse and cart or by bicycle. The butcher sent his delivery boy to the house with beef, mutton and pork.

◀ The cook carefully inspects some joints of meat, brought to the kitchen by the butcher's boy.

The poulterer supplied birds, such as geese, pigeons and larks. The grocer brought sugar, spices, tea, coffee and cocoa. The coalman delivered sacks of coal for the kitchen range and the other fires in the house. There were also crates of fish, packed in ice, from the fishmonger. All kinds of fish were eaten. Mrs Beeton's *Book of Household Management* (see below) includes 123 fish recipes, using 36 different types of fish.

During the Victorian period, new railway lines were built throughout most of Britain. Thanks to the railways, rich people in the countryside were able to order luxury foods from big London shops, such as Fortnum and Mason, which sent hampers loaded with wine, caviare, truffles and cans of turtle soup.

Tradesmen also visited the kitchen to buy waste products for recycling, such as bones and dripping (fat from roasted meat). Even old tea leaves were sold, and used again by the poor.

▲ Bills from the wine seller and the butcher. The housekeeper has paid the butcher £1 10s 6d (£1.52 in decimal money). At this time, a scullery maid would have earned about £8 a year, and a cook £30.

▶ Mrs Beeton's famous *Book of Household Management* (1861) was full of useful advice for cooks. Mrs Beeton included almost 2,000 recipes and also suggested menus for every month of the year. The pictures showed cooks how to display their dishes attractively.

11

PRESERVING FOOD

There were no freezers in Victorian houses. In order to make many foods last, they had to be specially prepared – by pickling, drying or salting. Victorian cooks spent almost as much time preserving foods as they did making meals.

Different foods were preserved at different times of the year. In June and July, strawberries, gooseberries and other soft fruits were boiled with sugar to make jam. Throughout the summer, vegetables, such as cauliflowers and onions, were pickled in vinegar. In the autumn, apples and pears were sliced into rings and dried in the kitchen range.

Joints of meat were preserved by rubbing them all over with salt. Another way of keeping meat or fish was to 'pot' it. It was cooked, cut up and put in a pot. Then it was covered with melted butter. When the butter cooled and set, it acted as a seal that protected the meat from the air.

◀ An ice chest, the nearest thing that the Victorians had to a refrigerator. Blocks of ice were placed inside next to the food. As the ice melted, the water was drawn off with the tap at the front. New ice had to be added every couple of days.

Meat in the kitchen had to be protected from flies – a big problem in hot weather. It was kept in a meat safe, a wooden box with a mesh door. The kitchen maids also hung sticky fly-papers from the kitchen ceiling and chased the flies with swatters.

◀ The cook and the upper kitchen maid are pickling onions and cauliflower florets. Cook pours vinegar into the jars. The maid seals the lids with sealing wax. When the wax cools it becomes hard again, sealing any gaps and stopping air getting into the jars.

▶ Preserved food was stored neatly on shelves in one of the larders.

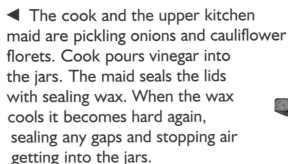

The simplest way of keeping things cool was to use 'clayware'. Earthenware covers, placed over bottles of milk, helped stop it going off. Rich Victorians also used ice to chill food. It was brought by horse and cart and stored in an ice-chest, or in a specially built underground ice-house, to stop it melting. The ice-chest was a box lined with asbestos or cork. Ice was used to keep fish fresh and to make ice-cream.

◀ Jams and preserves were also made by poorer people in the countryside.

BREAKFAST

Between 5 and 6 in the morning, the scullery maid and the kitchen maids woke up in their bedrooms in the attic. They dressed and made their way down through the cold dark house to the kitchen.

One kitchen maid remembered her first morning at work: *I was given a thick taper (candle) to light my way down the back stairs, and told not to put on my shoes, so as not to disturb anyone. I shall never forget the horror of that first morning, the crunch under my stockinged feet when I opened the kitchen door to find the floor and all about the fireplace thick with huge black beetles.*

While the kitchen maids swept the floor, the scullery maid began to clean and polish the range. Then she lit the coal fire and set a kettle to boil to make a pot of tea. The maids had some tea themselves and then took a cup upstairs to the cook.

▲ The scullery maid, still sleepy, polishes the range with black lead.

▶ Breakfast-time for the children. At the head of the table is the governess. She was employed by the family to teach the children, and make sure that they learned how to behave properly.

► Cups and saucers like these were used for breakfast and tea. This picture comes from a crockery manufacturer's catalogue.

At about 7 o'clock, the cook appeared and began to make breakfast for the family upstairs. This was a much bigger meal than most people eat today. All the dishes had to be quick and easy to prepare. The cook made curries and kedgerees, using meat and fish which had already been cooked. She fried eggs and bacon. She baked rolls, with dough which she had made the previous evening. There were also cold dishes, such as ham, tongue and pickled pork.

The food was taken upstairs to the dining room and placed on silver dishes on the sideboard. One by one, the family and their guests came in and helped themselves. Breakfast was the most relaxed meal in a Victorian house.

► The kitchen maids lay the table for breakfast.

FROM LUNCHEON TILL TEATIME

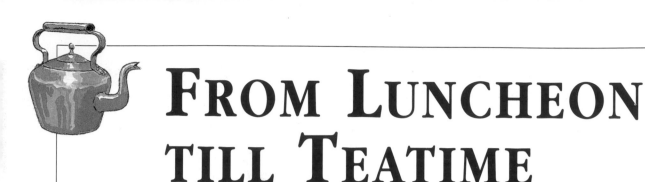

W hile the scullery maid was washing up the breakfast things, the next meals were being prepared in the kitchen. The cook left this work to the kitchen maids – she would need her energy for making the big evening meal.

▼ One of the lower kitchen maids butters bread for tea.

There were three meals to prepare at lunchtime. First was luncheon, served to the family upstairs at about one o'clock. Immediately afterwards, there was the servants' dinner, served in the servants' hall. Yet another meal, also called dinner, was sent to the children, upstairs in the nursery. Rich Victorians rarely ate with their children.

Luncheon was a light meal in which everything had to be attractively presented. There might be pies, hashed (finely chopped) meat and fruit tarts. The servants' dinner was very different. It was their main meal of the day and was made up of simple, filling dishes: boiled beef and mutton, rabbit stew, boiled vegetables and lots of bread. The nursery meals were both light and simple. By preparing such different styles of food, the maids learned many useful skills that would help them become cooks.

▲ A mustard advert. The picture shows some of the cold meats that might be served at luncheon.

▶ On sunny days a family picnic was a special treat.

▲ In the afternoon, rich Victorian ladies visited each other for tea and conversation. With servants to do all the work, they had plenty of free time.

In the afternoon, the kitchen maids had more work to do. They had to make afternoon tea, which was served upstairs by the housemaids at four o'clock. With the tea, the family and their guests ate cakes, thin slices of white bread and butter and toasted teacakes. Tea was also served in the nursery and to the servants. Dozens of pots of tea were brewed every day in the kitchen of the country house.

DINNER IS SERVED

First Course
Calf's-Head Soup
Brill and Shrimp Sauce
Broiled Mackerel

Entrées
Lobster Cutlets
Calf's Liver and Bacon

Second Course
Roast Loin of Veal
Two Boiled Fowls with
Béchamel Sauce
Boiled Knuckle of Ham
Spinach or Broccoli

Third Course
Wild Ducks
Apple Custards. Blancmange
Lemon Jelly. Jam Sandwiches
Ice-Pudding

Dessert and Ices

The cook's biggest task each day was to prepare dinner, the main meal of the day for the people upstairs. There were three main courses, each made up of three or four different dishes.

The first course was fish and soup. The second course was a selection of meats with vegetables. Between the two, there were the entrées, light fish or meat dishes. Then the third course combined game birds with puddings. Finally, there was a dessert of fruit and ices.

◄ The maids had to fold serviettes into different shapes, such as 'the fan open', shown here.

On the opposite page is a typical dinner menu for eight people. It comes from Mrs Beeton's book. Think of the work it took to cook this meal! Some things, such as puddings, could be made in advance, but the cook must have spent many hours standing over the hot range. She needed great skill to get the timing right. Everything had to be ready when it was needed. The kitchen maids helped by chopping ingredients and making sauces. They kept as quiet as they could while they worked, to avoid disturbing the cook.

Dinner was served by the footmen between 7 and 7.30. The butler was in charge of the wine. The family and guests wore evening dress – black tail coats for the men and beautiful gowns for the women. The children were already in bed.

With different cutlery and glasses for every course, the amount of washing-up could be enormous. The scullery maid washed the plates, pans and cutlery. The expensive glasses were washed by the footmen.

▼ At the sound of the dinner gong, the family and their guests gather for dinner. Look at all the different glasses, knives and forks!

◄ The look of every dish was as important as its taste, as this 1880 picture shows.

FESTIVE FOOD

One of the busiest times in the Victorian kitchen was Christmas, when everyone ate much more than usual. Just like today, certain dishes were always served at Christmas – mince pies, Christmas pudding and turkey.

▼ One of the lower kitchen maids has been making mince pies. The upper kitchen maid is mixing a pudding.

Christmas puddings were made days or weeks in advance. The kitchen maids mixed raisins, currants, almonds, beer, lemon peel, eggs, suet, sugar, spices and brandy together. They wrapped the mixture in a cloth or poured it into a buttered mould. It was then boiled for six hours. On Christmas day, the pudding was boiled again for two hours before it was served, decorated with a holly leaf. At the last minute, a glass of brandy was poured over the pudding and set alight.

Nowadays, people buy their turkeys ready to go into the oven. In Victorian times, a lot of extra work had to be done before cooking. After the turkey had been left hanging for a week in the game larder, its feathers were plucked by the scullery maid.

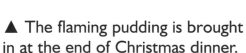

▼ A children's celebration, complete with party hats, watched over by a nursery maid.

A kitchen maid then chopped off its head and feet, and singed off any bristles with twisted burning paper. Then she pulled out the inner organs, taking care not to burst the gall-bladder, which would give the turkey a bitter taste. After this, she washed and wiped the bird, inside and out. Meanwhile, the cook was making forcemeat – a mixture of minced ham, bacon, suet, herbs and breadcrumbs. She stuffed this inside the turkey, which was then boiled in a pan of water or roasted in the oven.

▼ While cook stuffs the turkey, the scullery maid is thinking of all the washing up that lies ahead.

▲ The flaming pudding is brought in at the end of Christmas dinner.

The turkey was served with a sauce made from mushrooms, oysters or celery, accompanied by boiled ham, bacon, tongue and pickled pork.

THE END OF THE DAY

Once the huge dinner had been served, the cook could relax. It was left to the kitchen maids to make the last meal of the day, the servants' supper. This was a lighter meal than their dinner. It was eaten in the servants' hall, now lit by oil lamps.

▼ The servants sit down to their supper. Their long day is now almost over.

▼ Every evening, all over Britain, young maids had to do the washing up. This kitchen maid works for a poorer family, who can't afford a scullery.

Supper was described by a Victorian footman called William Taylor in his diary: 'At nine o'clock we have supper; this evening it's cold beef and damson pie. We keep plenty of good table ale in the house and everyone can have as much as they like.'

As they ate, the servants talked about all the things they had seen during the day, such as the behaviour of the rich people upstairs. For most of the servants, the day's work was over. But the kitchen maids and the scullery maid still had to clear away the supper things and do the washing-up. They were the last servants to go to bed, even though they had to be up first in the morning.

THE VICTORIAN DIET

Rich Victorians ate a varied and healthy diet; its main risk was the temptation to over-eat. Their servants ate more simply, but they never went hungry. Life was much harder for poorer people. Factory and farm workers lived on a diet of bread, cheese, bacon, potatoes and tea without milk – often made with old tea-leaves from the kitchens of the rich. The poorest of all went without the bacon and cheese. This diet, which had little protein and vitamins, made it hard for them to fight off the many diseases which swept through the slums of Victorian cities.

PLACES TO VISIT

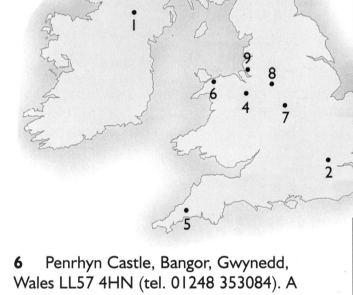

Many Victorian kitchens have been restored and are open to the public. This map shows where you can find some of the best.

1 The Argory, Dungannon, County Tyrone, Northern Ireland BT71 6NA (tel. 018678 84753). A beautifully decorated country house, built in the 1820s.

2 Carlyle's House, 24 Cheyne Row, Chelsea, London SW3 5HL (tel. 0171 352 7087). A four-storey town house with two small kitchens.

3 Cragside House, Rothbury, Morpeth, Northumberland NE65 7PX (tel. 01669 620333). The Victorian owners of Cragside bought every modern device for their kitchens, including an early gas stove.

4 Erddig, Wrexham, Clwyd, Wales LL13 OYT (tel. 01978 313333). An eighteenth-century house with a Victorian kitchen, still-room and pantries.

5 Lanhydrock, Bodmin, Cornwall PL30 5AD (tel. 01208 73320). A seventeenth-century house, rebuilt in 1881 after a fire. The kitchens, larders, scullery and other service rooms have hardly changed since.

6 Penrhyn Castle, Bangor, Gwynedd, Wales LL57 4HN (tel. 01248 353084). A mock castle, built in 1820–45, with an ice house and many service rooms.

7 Shugborough, Milford, Staffordshsire, ST17 OXB (tel. 01889 881388). A large country house with its own park. It includes a museum of everyday life, with live demonstrations of baking and brewing.

8 Tatton Park, Knutsford, Cheshire, WA16 6QN (tel. 01565 654822). The service rooms include a basement 'railway' for pushing trolleys of food down the long passages.

9 Speke Hall, The Walk, Liverpool L24 IXD (tel. 0151 427 7231). A Tudor house with a fully equipped Victorian kitchen and servants' hall.

INDEX

ale and beer 20, 22

Beeton, Mrs 11, 19
  *Book of Household
  Management* 11
birds 5, 10, 11, 18, 20–21
bread 16, 17, 23
breakfast 14–15, 16
butler 4, 19

children 4, 14, 16, 19, 21
Christmas 20–21
  dinner 20–21
  pudding 20
cooking methods
  baking 8
  boiling 8, 20, 21
  broiling 8
  frying 8
  poaching 9
  roasting 8, 21

dairy 7
dining room 6, 15
dinner 16, 18–19, 21, 22

fish 4, 6, 9, 11, 12, 13, 15, 18,
  21
footmen 3, 4, 19, 22
fruit 10, 12, 17, 18
  dried 20

game larder 10, 20
gardener 10

herbs 10, 21
housekeeper 4, 5, 6, 7, 11
housemaids 3, 4, 5, 17

ice 12–13

kitchen equipment 8–9, 19
  range 8, 9, 11, 12, 14, 19
kitchen staff 3
  cook 4, 5, 6, 12–13, 14, 15,
    16, 17, 18, 19, 21, 22
  lower kitchen maid 4, 5, 8, 9,
    13, 14, 15, 17, 19, 20, 21, 22
  upper kitchen maid 5, 9, 13,
    14, 15, 16, 17, 19, 20, 21, 22
  odd-job boy 4, 8
  scullery maid 4, 5, 7, 8, 11,
    14, 16, 19, 20, 21, 22

larders 6, 13
luncheon 16–17

meat 6, 10, 11, 12, 13, 15, 17,
  18
  bacon 15, 21, 23
  beef 17, 22
  bones 11
  chopped 17
  dripping 11

ham 15, 21
mutton 17
pork 15, 21
salted 12
tongue 15, 21
meat safe 13
milk 13, 23

nursery 16, 17

pies 5, 17, 20, 22
preserving food 12–13, 15
puddings 18, 19

recipe books 9, 11

sauces 18, 19, 21
scullery 5, 7, 22
spices 7, 9, 11, 20
still-room 7
storeroom 7
supper 22

teatime 16–17
tradesmen 10–11

vegetables 4, 5, 7, 10, 12, 13,
  17, 18, 21, 23
Victoria, Queen 3

washing-up 5, 7, 16, 19, 21, 22
wine 11, 19

PICTURE ACKNOWLEDGEMENTS

Bridgeman Art Library 13 (Bourne Art Gallery, Reigate), 17 top (Christopher Bourne Gallery, London), 17 bottom (Stapleton Collection), 21 middle (Private Collection), 22 (Musée des Beaux-Arts, Rouen); English Heritage Photographic Library 12; Image Select 19 bottom; Mary Evans Picture Library 11 top, 11 middle, 15, 19 top; National Trust Photographic Library 5 (John Hammond), 8 (Rob Matheson), 9 top (Andreas von Finsiedel); Robert Opie Collection 9 middle, 11 bottom, 14, 16 top, 21 top. The map on page 23 is by Peter Bull.